New Life Clarity Publishing

205 West 300 South, Brigham City, Utah 84302
Https://newlifeclarity.com/

Printed in the United States of America
ISBN- 978-0-578-57850-7
Library of Congress Control Number:2019918357
Copyright@2019

FINDING YOUR VOICE

Unlock Your Chains And Unleash Your Greatness

BY:
RENEE REISCH

"Renee's book is both relevant and relatable. Her storytelling draws you in and takes you along her journey. This book will help every reader discover their own powers and inspire them to take action. I know Renee personally, and when you read her book, you will get to know her too...and be glad you did."

Lynda Sunshine West
Executive Producer, Wish Man Movie, Founder of Living Live, Best Selling Author, Speaker, Mastermind & Accountability Coach

"Renee Reisch is one of those very unique people, that once you meet her, you think you have been best friends all of your life since birth. Her personality is vivacious; her charisma is infectious. Let her help you find your voice and be the motivation and inspiration that you need. Whether you are wildly successful, or starting a new enterprise, let Renee guide you to being more than you can be – let her guide you to a whole new level. I can't say enough about her, and once you meet her in person, you may indeed think I missed a few superlatives in describing her, because she left this indelible impression in your life; in your soul."

Tony DUrso
Author, & Host of the Tony DUrso Show on Voice America Influencers

"Renee Reisch is one of the most passionate, enthusiastic, caring people I know. She touches audiences deeply with her inspiring story of how she lost, then finally found her voice again. Renee truly connects with people and speaks from the heart. She is the ultimate networker. She generously spreads positive messages to her large social media network. I feel lucky to call her my friend."

Rita Connor
President Elite Resorts & Spas, Life & Professional Coach,
Certified Seminar Leader

"When I first met Renee, the connection was instant! It was no surprise then to learn that she had an innate gift and talent for making meaningful connections with everyone she met. Now Renee has taken her natural abilities and has poured her heart into a book that will help others grow and find their own voices. I am confident this book will create a connection with its readers, as well as provide positive support in their personal growth, because that is what Renee Reisch does."

Sheila Andres
CEO Realize Your Vision

"Renee is a ball of positivity! I have watched her through amazing challenges and adversity and she always finds a way to push through...and always with a smile. She has the ability to connect with people through her warmth and genuine caring."

Margaret Walker Scavo
MWS Executive Coaching

"Author Renee Reisch shares her journey to a better self. She shares stories and asks questions which allows the reader to ponder and to look inside themselves to help them discover how adversities are not a closed door on life. Renee explains how her physical adversity brought happiness, confidence and opportunities into her life beyond her imagination! An excellent read and Renee's "can do" attitude is contagious!"

Nancy Gross
Retired Teacher and Friend

"Renee's positivity and enthusiasm shine through everything she touches. She's a genuine, honest, and nurturing angel whose generosity and kindness is contagious. Her passion for making meaningful connections with people is inspiring. You're going to love this book!"

Britt Wilson
Team Lead/Trainer Lincoln Experience Center, President B. Braun Toastmasters, Workshop Facilitator Women Helping Women

"Renee Reisch has been a light of strength and resilience in my life. She has taught me that using my voice has so much to do with the value I have for myself. I live by her quote "It's all how you say it.""

Danielle Rocco Roc LLC
Relationship Expert

"The moment I met Renee, I knew she was someone special. I was speaking at an event where she was an attendee, and while I was on stage gazing the room, my eyes locked in on her exuberant smile. Renee approached me after my interview and from that day forward, we became friends. Renee is a supporter, she's a connector, and for those who don't know her very well, should know that she's overcome tremendous adversity that has helped shape the person that she is today. You can tell that Renee has a mission, and that's to tell her story so that others will be inspired to find their voice and to share their story as well. I assure you that reading *Finding Your Voice: Unlock Your Chains and Unleash Your Greatness*, will be a transformational moment in your life."

Dupé Aleru
Motivational Speaker & Content Creator

"Renee is a rare gem and her personal story of loss and leading a life worth living is a true treasure that will enlighten and enrich anyone who reads this book. Take a journey along with her and receive the gift of finding your own voice!"

Mike Gellman
CEO, High Five Career Coach, Author

"It's our inner voice that creates the fear, and our outer voice that overcomes it. Renee guides the reader to find their inner voice in a very straight forward approach. You'll feel richly rewarded as you absorb the valuable information she offers throughout the book."

Dean Levin
CEO-Founder Wake Up Wine Inc.

Foreword by Tamara Hunter

FINDING YOUR VOICE:
Unlock Your Chains and Unleash Your Greatness

Book by Renee Reisch

"Renee has found a beautiful way of crafting a message needed by many. This book will transform your life. Follow her lead, do the work, and you will find the voice that has always been within you is now ready to be shared with your family, your community, your world."

Tamara Hunter, Executive Director & Co-founder of Chemo Buddies 4life, The Service Heroes Show Creator and Host, and the World's First Next Impactor

ABOUT THE AUTHOR

 Renee has cultivated and inspired individuals and teams for over a decade. You immediately feel her energy when she enters a room. After 25 years working in a Fortune 500 Company, she decided it was time to hang up the corporate ladder and put on her running shoes.

Born in New York and raised in New Jersey, Renee knew her east coast grit would resonate with audiences seeking to improve their lives and their careers. She started her professional training and speaking at Women Helping Women, a non-profit organization, where she donated her time helping the unemployed and underemployed find and keep their jobs.

Renee has received numerous awards over the years for bringing her teams to the number one position. Both her years, and expertise in retail have taught her that in order to move the bar and increase profit, you must first invest in people.

A motivational speaker, transformational coach, and influencer, Renee loves connecting with female entrepreneurs and speakers seeking to gain more confidence to become the leaders they are meant to be.

After suffering a devastating illness that took away her voice, she lost her best friend and then father. Renee decided to follow her friend's example to never give up. Now, that legacy is how Renee has chosen to live her life and help others, showing them that just when they feel life is closing in on them, there is always a way out.

DEDICATION

This book is dedicated to my best friend in heaven who taught me to never give up and what the true meaning of friendship is all about.

To my father, who passed during the writing of this book, and taught me to always "keep the faith" and about Tikkun Olam, "Repair The World."

To my mother, who has shown by her example how to move forward in the face of adversity and not dwell on what was, but focus on what is. Her love, support, and belief in me when I sometimes didn't believe in myself has meant more than I can ever express. When times were tough, she was there to lend an ear and with words of wisdom and encouragement as only a mother can give.

To my brothers, and sister-in-law who stood by me without judgement, but with love, I will always be grateful.

To my many coaches, and mentors along the way, I appreciate you and am glad you were there to help guide me on my journey. Finally, thank you to my fellow entrepreneurs and friends who know the road less traveled may not be the easiest, but is the most rewarding. I am grateful to each and every one of you, and thankful you are in my life.

TABLE OF CONTENTS

Introduction

❧❧❧

FINDING YOUR VOICE UNLOCK YOUR CHAINS AND UNLEASH YOUR GREATNESS

When I first began this journey, I never imagined I would be writing a book. It first came to me from a long- time family friend on the East Coast who, during a conversation said "you should write a book." I knew she was serious. That was over two years ago. Since that time, I have been receiving "nudges" through multiple sources telling me the very same thing. I kept putting it to the back burner thinking it would take too much time. I was looking for work and didn't think I could nor should devote *that* kind of time to it. Then, whenever I went on Facebook another friend was out there promoting his or her book and not only had they promoted their first book, but some were on to their second and even their third! As happy as I was for each of them, I too had a story to tell and now is the time for me to finally use my voice and tell it.

Chapter 1

❦❦

MY BEST FRIEND

"Cherish your human connections-your
relationships with friends and family."
~Barbara Bush~

Have you ever had a friend or someone in your life who loved you and believed in you so much, that even during those times you didn't believe in yourself, she did? For me, that was my friend, Lynne. She wasn't just any friend, she was my best friend in the world, my soul sister. We did everything together, and nothing together, but it was just being together that made all the difference in the world. Although we created many memories, the biggest attribute my best friend imparted upon me however, wasn't a memory at all, but rather her legacy to never give up and make sure you have someone in your corner in the process.

A prime example of this happened in December of 2013 while I was a manager for a very large retail corporation. I had gone to work sick, but knowing I was the only senior manager scheduled to close that night, I felt compelled to stay. I remember walking out to my car at 1:00 a.m., shivering and barely able to swallow, just looking forward to getting into bed. The next morning, I drove myself to Urgent Care. I told the doctor I felt like I had a sore in my throat as opposed to a regular sore throat. My feeling was confirmed. She said there was one big one sitting smack in the center. I tested negative for strep, but due to the infection, I was running a low-grade fever.

The next morning, I felt even worse. My best friend Lynne picked me up and drove me back to Urgent Care. My one sore had apparently given birth overnight to many. When I asked the doctor how many, she would not say. She knew me well enough to know I would freak out. That alone said it all. She told us to go straight to the emergency room. Knowing how long a wait it would be, Lynne decided to stop at her house along the way to pick up a few things. I stood in her living room as she quickly maneuvered around the house. She packed extra socks, snacks, magazines and a blanket. She made me laugh amidst my pain. I asked if she thought we were going on a picnic or something. She said she wanted to make sure we had everything we might need. Being a former Girl Scout, she was *always* prepared. While in the ER, I was tested for several diseases, some of which made me feel like I was back in the time of "Little House on the Prairie." Laying on the bed there I remember asking the doctor if I was contagious. He looked down at me and spoke the following words I will never forget. "Oh, you're highly contagious, you can't be with the public." Those words hit me like a ton of bricks! How could this be? The two things I love most in this world aside from G-d and my family, are speaking and the ability to connect with others. Those were the very two things that were taken away. What did I do wrong? Why was I being punished?

I didn't understand. I was given a spray to numb my throat and told to follow up with my primary care physician. After a bunch of bloodwork, I was diagnosed with a highly contagious disease known as viral pharyngitis. If I was to go out, I had to wear a mask and if anyone was to visit me, they were to do the same. The only one who ever did visit was my best friend Lynne. She would come by several times during the week to drop off applesauce, Gatorade, Jell-O, soup, and kosher chicken she cooked...just the way I liked it. She told me I needed protein to keep up my strength. Lynne also always included the latest issue of *Cosmo* or *People* she felt I would enjoy. She even brought over coloring books and crayons. She said it would help keep me relaxed and focus my mind on something other than myself. She was right.

This illness was not only the beginning of a three and

a half- month leave of absence from my career, but the beginning of learning to survive in a world of isolation where I could no longer be heard. It robbed me of my voice AND made me a prisoner in my own home. It was like a jail cell *slamming* down on a cold cement floor! Welcome to my world.

Takeaway

**Think of a time in your life when you felt overwhelmed
or out of control. What physical ailment took place? __**

_____

_____

_____

_____

_____

_____

_____

_____

_____

_____

_____

_____

_____

_____

_____

_____

_____

_____

Finding Your Voice

_____

_____

_____

_____

_____

_____

_____

_____

_____

_____

_____

_____

_____

_____

_____

_____

_____

_____

_____

Renee Reisch

Chapter 2

❧❧❧

SUNRISE/SUNSET

"Where there is love, there is life."
~Mahatma Gandhi~

Days and nights went by with no change in sight. There seemed to be no light at the end of the tunnel, just the depth of darkness inside. That darkness led to depression.

I remember sitting on my couch, staring outside the window and watching the days go by. Usually several times during the week, I would see Lynne's car coming up the driveway. Seeing her lifted my heart and spirit. She worked three jobs, yet *always* made room in her day to take care of me. She would come up my stairs wearing a face mask along with a bag or two filled with easy to swallow foods and magazines to read. Due to the intensity of the pain in swallowing, eating was not something I looked forward to. I knew I needed nourishment, but when it is difficult to swallow your own saliva, the mere thought of having to swallow anything else wreaked havoc on my mind. Although it was extremely painful, the love behind it was stronger.

Since most people I associated with at that time knew I was sick, I seldom received any calls. Aside from telemarketers, Dr. T, my primary care physician, was it. For obvious reasons, I always let it go to voicemail. They were messages directing me to go for more bloodwork. My doctor kept trying to peel back the layers of the onion to figure out why I wasn't getting better. She reasoned that if she was able to find *something*, she could at least begin to treat it, but it kept taking her back to square one. Due to the fact that this was a viral infection, there was nothing she could prescribe for me to take. Plain and simple, I had contracted a virus that required time packed with a load of patience to heal itself.

I quickly learned that patience was not my strongest attribute. The toughest part was not being able to do anything to speed up the healing process. As I write this, however, I now realize that is what got me there in the first place. I was always running around at warp speed. Lynne would tell me to slow down and breathe, but I never listened. Now I was forced to.

Takeaway

Where are three places in your life you can have more patience? If you can't come up with three, shoot for one. Take a minute to think about this. Be honest. _____

_____

_____

_____

_____

_____

_____

_____

_____

_____

_____

_____

_____

_____

_____

_____

_____

Chapter 3

❧❧❧❧

THE LIGHT

"The difference between try and triumph
is a little umph."
~Author Unknown~

By the end of the three and a half months, my doctor sent me to a voice specialist to see if there was any permanent damage to my vocal cords. That was a scary trip! Would I ever speak again? Would I ever be able to thank Lynne for being there for me through it all and tell her how grateful I was and how much I love her? Would I be able to tell Mom and Dad and my brothers I love them?

I sat in a chair with what appeared to be a large flat screen TV above me. Two doctors in white coats came over with a long tube and small camera attached to the end. They explained that they were going to put it down my throat to get a better look at my vocal cords. This may be how they would view their findings, but it is NOT how I ever envisioned making it to "The Big Screen!" Google what your vocal cords look like, you will be amazed! They asked me to make what little sound I could to make an assessment. A faint whisper mixed with a squeaky little noise came out...eeee, ahhhh, ohhhh. Then was the BIG REVEAL! My heart was in my stomach! The doctor told me there did *not* appear to be permanent damage! I wanted to shout from the rooftop!! HALLELUJAH!! AMEN!! I was told I would need to go to a vocal coach to retrain and strengthen my voice again. That was music to my ears!! I could do that!! I wanted to cry; in fact, I think I did.

Takeaway

Recall a time in your life when you overcame an obstacle. What steps did you take? What was the result? _____

_____

_____

_____

_____

_____

_____

_____

_____

_____

_____

_____

_____

_____

_____

_____

_____

Finding Your Voice

Renee Reisch

_____

_____

_____

_____

_____

_____

_____

_____

_____

_____

_____

_____

_____

_____

_____

_____

_____

_____

_____

_____

Chapter 4

ՉՀՀՉ

THE ROAD TO RECOVERY

"Maybe life isn't about avoiding the bruises.
Maybe it's about collecting the scars to prove
that we showed up for it."
~Hannah Brencher~

I was referred to a local voice coach by Dr. T. Her name was Michelle. She was great! She had the voice of an angel and was always so calming and reassuring. She told me she knew she could help me, but I had to do the work. There was a lot!! Michelle used the voice memo on her cell phone to show me what she wanted me to do. She would do the exercise first and I was to repeat it. She wanted to see how long I could hold different sounds before my voice went out. It was very brief. I was never pitch perfect, but the more I practiced, the longer I was able to hold the sound. It was similar to not working out for an extended period of time. Your muscles will atrophy. In this case, it was my vocal muscles. So, I needed to start working them out once again. My homework was to look in the mirror daily and do the various exercises assigned to me while using my phone to record. Talk about taking a look in the mirror! It wasn't pretty, but I was determined to make it happen. Day after day, week after week eeee.... ahhhh.... ohhhhh. A friend suggested I look on YouTube to add to my repertoire of exercises, so I did. I incorporated those exercises along with my existing ones. Since I was told this was not a permanent situation and I was able to heal, I wanted to do everything possible to get better. I knew if it was to be it was up to me. Michelle and I would meet once a week. She was happy with my progress. I recall receiving a text from her one morning while getting ready for our appointment. Michelle was on her way to the hospital to give birth to her new baby girl! I had a feeling she was going to be reaching much higher octaves that day than I ever would. For a brief moment, I selfishly wanted to get to my appointment with her before she went in for hers, but I knew there was a new life waiting to come out into the world and a new voice to be heard.

I continued working on my vocal exercises daily while Michelle took on the role of motherhood. They weren't fun, but I knew the sooner my voice got stronger, the stronger and more confident I too would become. Michelle took a very brief maternity leave prior to returning. We continued our work together for a few more months before I was on my own. I now had the necessary tools to pull from my toolbox whenever I needed them. I will always be grateful to Michelle for helping me regain my voice.

Takeaway

Think back to a time when you lost your voice. This may be physically or metaphorically. What happened? How did you resolve the issue (or is it still going on?)

Is there something or somewhere in your life where you need help?

Do not be afraid to seek support from a specialist. That is why they are called specialists. They have the knowledge and knowhow to take you from point A to point B. Do not hold back. Remember, this exercise is for YOU! _____

_____

_____

_____

_____

_____

_____

_____

_____

_____

_____

_____

_____

Renee Reisch

Chapter 5

❧❧❧❧

OLD HABITS DIE HARD

"We are what we repeatedly do. Excellence,
therefore, is not an act but a habit."
~Aristotle~

I recall my first day back on the job. I remember seeing my boss walking about fifty feet in front of me in the parking lot. I was unable to call out to her because my voice was still so weak. I managed to catch up to her as quickly as I could. I broke down in tears. I hadn't been there in over three months, and as much as people tend to complain about their jobs, it was just good to be back with people again. My first day at work was like the first day of school. Butterflies were flying all around my stomach! I was both nervous and scared. Nervous because I knew my job was very demanding and required me to speak, and scared because I didn't know if I would be able to perform it at the level I was used to. I needed to get out of my own head and just go with whatever happened.

Everyone was very nice and welcomed me back. Half way through my second day I remember walking up the stairs and feeling very dizzy. I ended up almost fainting in one of my co-manager's arms. He brought me to the Executive Office. The next thing I knew, I was out of work for another few weeks. Back to the doctor's office again. She told me my dizziness was due to a middle ear infection. My desire to return to work was there, but my body had not yet caught up. More rest, more quiet time, and more time to reflect inward. Time seems to be the very thing we are always seeking, yet when we are forced to take it due to illness, it seems endless. I did not enjoy being alone, yet once again this is where I found myself.

The night before I was to return to work for the second time, my best friend Lynne sat down with me to make sure that *this* time I would be ready. I remember sitting opposite her in the living room and paying close attention as she spoke. She told me to take it slow, drink plenty of water, take breaks as needed and *leave on time!* I used to stay way past my shifts because there was always so much to do. Lynne knew this and always got frustrated with me. She had already witnessed first-hand the effect all the overtime had on me and was *not* about to have it happen again! When you are salaried, no one chases you out.

I returned to work and went about my day with Lynne's words in my head. I even promised G-d I would do better! I knew I could have done a better job at taking breaks, but felt guilty if I had. Heck, I'd been on a break for almost four months and my co-managers had to pick up all the extra slack while I was away. The *last* thing I wanted them to see was me sitting down! I was concerned about what others would think instead of what was best for me. I stuck to leaving on time for the *most* part and not working from home *too* much as I had done before. Then slowly but surely, my old habits began resurfacing. I would stay late at work, eat dinner with Lynne on my early shifts, then stay up till midnight or later working on schedules for my teams. I figured the more I got done at home, the more time I would be able to spend coaching and developing my teams at work. I was running through life once again. I would look forward to my days off, not because they were "days off," but because I would be able to accomplish more work before my next scheduled shift. I was constantly trying to stay ahead of the rat race to see how much more work I could accomplish in a day. I felt like a hamster on one of those hamster wheels.

Takeaway

Think of a time when you promised to change a behavior that was no longer serving you and your old habits came creeping back in. What was the result? This is not a time to berate yourself, we are all human. It is just an exercise for you to see that *you* are in control. No one is running the show but you. If you want to see a change, *you* are the one who is responsible for making it happen...and you can. _____

_____

_____

_____

_____

_____

_____

_____

_____

_____

_____

_____

_____

_____

_____

Finding Your Voice

_____

_____

_____

_____

_____

_____

_____

_____

_____

_____

_____

_____

_____

_____

_____

_____

_____

_____

_____

Chapter 6

❦❦❦

THE YEAR OF LOST AND FOUND

"What lies behind us and what lies before us are tiny matters compared to what lies within us."
~Ralph Waldo Emerson~

It has been over five and a half years since I was so sick. The saying "if G-d brings you to it, he will bring you through it" really resonates with me.

There were lessons I needed to learn since losing my voice in 2013. First, to be a better listener. After all, we have two ears and one mouth, and second, to be a leader and empower others, especially women to use their voice. I have attended several women's events. After speaking at one of them, a few women approached me saying that they too had experienced losing their voice. They had to do with relationships where these women did not speak up. When we don't express ourselves, it can manifest into our lives as physical ailments. Whether it is in your job, your home or your marriage, communication is key. I now believe losing my voice was because I didn't use my voice. I seldom, if ever, spoke up in any area of my life, whether it was personal or business. I felt it was more important for me to please others and be liked than to go against the grain. I now know that not everyone will always like me, or agree with me, and that's ok. The people who are supposed to be in my life will be, and that is what matters.

I have had the pleasure and privilege of using my voice at a multitude of events since that time such as: Women of Achievement aboard the Queen Mary, Millionaire Speaker Summit, and Women of Influence. I have also attended several Global Women's conferences where I was able to share my voice with others.

I was asked to speak at an event in San Diego hosted by a friend. It was only a four-minute spot, but I was grateful for the opportunity. I practiced that speech like I was going to be the keynote speaker, while standing in front of my mirror, over and over and over. All my practice paid off, as a woman watching from Seattle via Facebook Live had reached out and told me she felt I was speaking directly to her. You never know the impact you will have on another. As I learned from Arvee Robinson, Master Speaker Trainer, International Speaker and Author, "words become worlds."

During my friend's event, there was a raffle drawing to attend another event where Jack Canfield was scheduled to speak. Two winners were to be drawn. Each ticket was valued at $1500! Something inside of me said I was going to be one of those winners. We were asked to text a word to a specific number. My fingers were ready...and *GO*...I didn't know I could text so fast with long nails but I did it...I WON!!! WOO HOO!! My feeling was right! I had Jack Canfield on my vision board for the past year and really wanted to attend. Now it was actually going to happen!! (A vision board is a collage of various images which can include quotes, pictures or images that represent your goals. It is a great visualization tool). In the midst of my excitement, I suddenly realized the other expenses involved with not only traveling to, but attending this event. I had absolutely no idea how I would make it happen with such short notice and just gave it to G-d. I have been told on numerous occasions, you need to know the "what" and the "why" and let the Universe figure out the "how." The following day, I attended a Global Women's Luncheon in Los Angeles. I had invited a lot of friends to join me. Dr. Marlena was one of them. I hadn't seen her the entire day. Then as luck would have it, we saw each other on our way out. I asked if she enjoyed the day and if she was planning on going to San Diego for the Author Millionaire

Live Weekend Event where Jack would be speaking. She said she had a great time and was planning on attending. I then asked if she wanted to share a room. Take note, the Universe is always listening and conspiring for our highest good. Dr. Marlena said she had already booked a room, but I was welcome to share it with her. I couldn't believe it! Not that she offered, because she has such a huge heart, but the good karma that was being returned to me. I didn't even know about the San Diego event when I initially invited her to the Los Angeles one. Had we not run into each other, that never would have happened. We were friends, yes, but because we were both in the same entrepreneurial space, we typically only saw each other at events throughout the year. The irony in the fact that she too was going to be attending *and* had her reservations booked was incredible! I graciously accepted her generosity in offering to share her room with me. There was my "how."

Takeaway

Recall a time in your life when you wanted to do something but didn't know how it would happen, then by some wonderful twist of fate, it did. This is an exercise on gratitude. Too often we take things for granted and don't truly give thanks for what took place or the blessings we received. _____

_____

_____

_____

_____

_____

_____

_____

_____

_____

_____

_____

_____

_____

Renee Reisch

_____

_____

_____

_____

_____

_____

_____

_____

_____

_____

_____

_____

_____

_____

_____

_____

_____

_____

_____

_____

_____

Finding Your Voice

Renee Reisch

Chapter 7

❧❦❧

EXPOSED

"Whatever you want in life, other people are going to want it too. Believe in yourself enough to accept the idea that you have an equal right to it."
~Diane Sawyer~

Sunday, January 20, 2019, the day I will always remember. It finally happened! One of the few things I had remaining on my vision board since last January was meeting Jack Canfield! I had won the $1500 ticket to the Author Millionaire Live Weekend Event while attending my friend's event the prior weekend.

Day one was filled with many great speakers, including Steve Harrison, the gentleman who helped Jack Canfield publish his Chicken Soup for the Soul series. I had heard him speak on his podcasts and received his newsletters, but never thought I would be in the same room with him taking pictures together!

Then came Sunday. We were told the doors would open at 8:30 a.m. sharp so we made sure to get there on time. When we arrived, the doors were still closed. Since there were not many people there yet, I was able to walk right to the front. I made small talk with a gentleman in line as well as with a gentleman working the event. As we were speaking, I could have sworn I caught a glimpse of Jack through a slit in the door. Could it be? Was I *that* close to this man I had been following for so long? Reading his books, watching him on YouTube, even putting him on my vision board! I resumed talking with those around me, when moments later one door opened. There he was! JACK CANFIELD, right in front of my face! I made sure not to sound like a blubbering fool. In fact, I had played out the scenario in my head just a few days before. He was on his way somewhere, but still stopped to speak with me as he realized I was not going to let this opportunity pass me by. I said: "Jack (like he was my good friend or something), I've had you on my vision board for a year!" He smiled and said, "now you can take me off." I asked for a photo. He said he needed to take care of something (which was why he originally stepped out before I stopped him in his tracks), but promised me one after. When the doors finally opened to let us in, I stuck close by Jack. I saw others walking up to him for pictures and didn't want to push my way through. I was about to retreat to my seat when a woman watching me took my cell phone and said: "No, get in there! You're going to get your picture!" So, I did. I never got her name, but am very grateful to her for making it happen.

Dr. Marlena, my good friend and roommate for the weekend, had gone to the car to get an extra shawl we were going to share to keep us warm. They keep the rooms cold to make sure we stay awake, but boy was it freezing!

After Lunch, Jack was still on stage giving his presentation. During his talk, he held up one of his many books, *The Success Principles*, which I had been wanting. I actually had his team hold one for me before our break, but because we needed to check out of the hotel by 1:00 pm, I used that time to settle our bill. I never got to purchase the book after lunch, because by the time we got back the event had already started. I had no idea he would be giving away this particular book during his talk. I was sitting three rows from the stage and saw it in his hands. I thought: NOW is your chance Renee. Get up there!! If you really want something, you've got to take massive action! I quickly removed all the sweaters I had covering me to keep warm and ran up. My adrenaline was pumping! When I got to the front of the stage, I found myself standing on the floor looking up at him with my hands clasped behind my back and my head down like a demure little flower. The audience chuckled as they watched me patiently waiting for Mr. Canfield to give me the book. Then all of a sudden, a very tall aggressive woman came running up behind me and grabbed it from his hands. How could she? I turned around and gasped! It was the "nice" woman who just the day before had gotten out of her seat to get me water when she heard me coughing. How could this kind soul turn on me like this? I was mortified! The anger and frustration in me took over. That demure sweet girl standing with her hands behind her back in front of the stage facing Jack Canfield, turned and chased this woman to her seat. Two could play *that* game! If she was going to play rough, then so was I! I tried to grab it back from her but could not. I went back to my seat feeling both dejected and embarrassed. A man in the audience started a chant with his fist in the air saying: "Give her the book! Give her the book!" Jack asked how many people wanted that book and hands went up. He said, "yet no one but these two ladies came to get it...well almost." I started defending my actions from my seat. The mic was brought over to me. I said: "I wanted to be respectful while you were speaking and would not have wanted someone to grab a book out of my hands as I was giving a presentation." Jack asked; "and how did that work out for you?" I said, "apparently it didn't." He said "and what did you learn?" I said, "to be more aggressive and assertive." What happened shortly after was another lesson. Jack continued his talk as I calmed myself down. I still couldn't believe this woman had done this to me. But truthfully, *she* hadn't done anything to me. I had done it to *myself*. A few minutes went by. During the presentation she got out of her seat and brought the book to me. I turned back around. She mouthed telling me to read the note she had written inside. I opened the cover and took it out. It said, "I didn't plan on keeping it. I want you to recognize your value." She drew a happy face next to her words. Then signed it "With Love, Vicky." During the break I went over to a gentleman from Jack's team to let him know I no longer needed the book to be held. He said, "I know, I saw." He then said "where else is this showing up in your life?" Boy, was I ever exposed! My stomach sank as I pondered that question. Just like books on a shelf, it was apparent that my lack of self-confidence and self-esteem were out there for everyone to see.

I then found Vicky and thanked her for the book and her note. She put her hands on my shoulders, looked me in the eyes and said: "I don't want to hurt you by what I'm about to say (uh oh *now* what was she going to tell me?), but I want you to know you are enough! I know you are working on yourself." I nodded in agreement. She said, "you need to know your value." Vicky autographed one of her books for me and in it she wrote: "OWN who you are and recognize your value! #YouAreEnough!" She signed her name with a heart then wrote #RockThatDream! I plan on it,

Vicky. I suppose being called out on "your stuff" in front of Jack Canfield and over one hundred authors, producers and speakers is what it took for me to get my ass back in the chair and continue writing this book.

Takeaway

Recall a time when you felt something was wrongfully taken away from you. How did you feel? What did you do? What was the result? Take this time to seriously reflect upon the situation and write down what took place both emotionally and physically. When we reflect upon situations we are not pleased with, it gives us an opportunity to use each one as a learning experience. Every experience affords growth.

_____

_____

_____

_____

_____

_____

_____

_____

_____

_____

_____

_____

_____

Renee Reisch

Finding Your Voice

Renee Reisch

Chapter 8

ﮎﮌﮎ

WHAT'S IN A NAME?

"Bee to the blossom, moth to the flame;
Each to his passion; what's in a name?"
~Helen Hunt Jackson~

In addition to attending events, I have also used my voice to connect with and interview some highly recognizable and respected individuals including: Post-War Veterans; Frank Shankwitz, Co-Founder of Make-A-Wish Foundation, recipient of the President's Call to Service Award, Making a World of Difference Award, Ellis Island Medal of Honor Award, and Doctor of Philosophy Degree; Sir John Shin, Producer of Think and Grow Rich Legacy World Tour and Author at the Napoleon Hill Foundation; Dr. Marissa Pei, Motivational Speaker, TV Commentator and Radio Personality; and Forbes Riley, World Renowned Fitness and

Wellness Expert, National Fitness Hall of Fame Inductee, the Number One Infomercial Host in the country, Founder of SpinGym, as well as Actress and Producer, just to name a few. I have also interviewed people such as: Reverend Prince Adekoya of Nigeria and had the pleasure of meeting and spending time with Shea Vaughn, CEO of WWTVN and OTT Network, a bestselling author, producer and nationally recognized as "America's Queen of Wellness" authority. These individuals have all worked very hard to achieve the levels of success they have reached. They are still going strong and continue to grow and make a difference in our world.

So, what's in a name? That all depends on the value you give to it. The people I mentioned above are wonderful, yes, but it's not to brag about who I have met or what I have done. This isn't about me, or them for that matter, but rather to let you know that you too can do anything you set your mind to. They are ordinary people just like you and me. They did not wake up with a silver spoon in their mouth. It took years of hard work and determination to get to where they are today. With a little perseverance, you too can achieve whatever it is YOU want to do.

Takeaway

What is one thing you have wanted to do but haven't because you didn't think you could?

What or who is standing in your way of making it happen? Be aware, the *who* may very well be you. Is there anyone you know to assist you in achieving it? Start making a list of people you can reach out to who might be able to help. If you don't know anyone, maybe some of your contacts do. I've had friends connect me via social media with their friends if they didn't have all the answers I needed and I have done the same for them. My point being, there *is* a way to move forward. _____

_____

_____

_____

_____

_____

_____

_____

_____

_____

_____

_____

Chapter 9

✿✿✿✿

PERFECTLY IMPERFECT

"In the middle of a difficulty lies opportunity."

~Albert Einstein~

I received a message from my friend Lynda asking if I would interview her regarding an upcoming movie that was soon to be released. She was one of the executive producers and was working diligently to get the word out there for this film. I wanted to support her efforts and agreed. We set up a time and date. She asked what platform I would be using and I said, "Facebook Live." She suggested I use Stream Yard for Facebook because it would come across better to our audience. I had been on other's Facebook Lives as a guest using Stream Yard, but never as the host. The prior weekend I googled it and went through the tutorial to make sure I was ready. I practiced adding banners and posting comments from our viewers; everything I felt would add value to the broadcast. The morning of our scheduled interview I messaged Lynda so we could chat for fifteen or twenty minutes in advance to review both the platform as well as any specifics she wanted to discuss. We were ready. I counted us down. "Going live in five, four, three, two, one and we are live!" The interview lasted about fifty minutes. We received great support from our audience with hearts and thumbs up throughout. Everything was great *except* for the fact that I left the broadcast before clicking the red "leave broadcast button" when it ended. Lynda messaged me to let me know we were still live! My feeling of joy for having such a successful interview quickly turned into panic! I was in flight or fight mode. I had signed off with our audience, said good-bye, and clicked off the broadcast, *but* what I hadn't realized is just because you "x out" of an application, it doesn't necessarily mean you have exited it. I began to sweat and asked Lynda how I could fix it...fast! I was mortified!! She said she told the audience I left the broadcast. OMG!! Here I was promoting a huge film with one of the executive producers who believed in me to do a great job. I felt like I let her down and everyone else watching. Lynda had another call to get to and could no longer help me "fix" the problem. I immediately called and messaged friends in various parts of the country asking for help. One of them told me I could "hide" the interview until it was edited then repost. Another friend felt my panic and had me send him the interview in an email. Since it lasted close to an hour, he told me it would take twenty minutes to download. Twenty minutes?! It seemed like forever! During the interim, we face-timed. He decided to show me his home and take me on a tour outside to see his backyard and the beautiful ocean he lived so close to. He knew he had to somehow calm me down and focus on anything other than what had happened while the file I sent him was downloading. After my twenty-minute tour of his home and the beautiful scenery, he realized the video could not be edited. My panic set back in.

I called my friend Tamara in San Diego. *She* always did Facebook Lives! *She* would know what to do! She said she never used the platform I was on; however, she knew there was a way to edit and "hide" it! Whew! That was great news. She told me how to do it and I did. The interesting thing was that each time I logged onto Facebook it said there were more views on the video. I thought, "how could that be?" I hid it. Well, I *thought* I had. Apparently when the video is on your timeline, you can't necessarily hide it from other places it might show up. The saying, "you can run, but you can't hide" is exactly how I felt. When I told Lynda I hid it until I could figure out a way for it to be edited, she asked, "why?" She said she makes mistakes all the time publicly, then asked if I wanted to edit it for *me* or for my *audience*?

It was certainly something to think about. The irony of the whole situation was that during the interview I spoke about being perfectly imperfect and failing forward. Ya think the Universe heard? I didn't mean for it to happen to *me!* Therein lies the problem and an immediate call to action. I had said it's ok and stated publicly about not needing to be perfect, yet as soon as it happened to me, I freaked out and tried to hide my own mistake. Lynda suggested I post about it with our interview. I proceeded to follow her sound advice, making an addendum to the post and letting the audience know what happened...unapologetically.

Takeaway

What was the advice that you gave someone, yet when it happened to you, it suddenly didn't apply? Be brutally honest here. Remember, in order to grow we must own our imperfections and be ok with them. It is part of being human. _____

_____

_____

_____

_____

_____

_____

_____

_____

_____

_____

_____

_____

_____

_____

_____

_____

Renee Reisch

Finding Your Voice

_____

_____

_____

_____

_____

_____

_____

_____

_____

_____

_____

_____

_____

_____

_____

_____

_____

_____

_____

Renee Reisch

Chapter 10

❧❧❧❧

FAILING FORWARD

"Tell me, and I forget. Teach me, and I remember.
Involve me, and I learn."
~Benjamin Franklin~

T he day was Monday. The date was February 4, 2019. I
remember this because it was a day my mother wasn't
very pleased with me. I knew I had done something wrong.
During one particular visit with mom after dad passed, she
was on the phone in his old office trying to get in touch with
a human being at the bank. I overheard her having what
seemed to be a very frustrating experience. Press 1 for this, 2
for that, 3 if you want this *and* that...it went on and on. I got
up from my desk, walked into the office and took the phone
from her to try and help. I was going to push all the right
buttons in an effort to get to the person she wanted...or *any*

person for that matter. The one wrong button I pushed was Mom's. I knew I had overstepped my boundaries. Here she was taking care of things that needed to be done; and there I was thinking I could do better. My stomach sank as I glanced over and saw the look of frustration on her face. I realized what I had done. Instead of allowing Mom to do what she set out to accomplish, I stepped in. I was taken aback by what had just happened as I now heard that frustration come through her voice. She clearly explained that if I continued doing everything for her, she would never know if she could manage on her own. Quite frankly, nor would I. She was right. I handed the phone back to her to complete the call. Although my intervention didn't exactly go as intended, it didn't completely backfire either. There was a lesson. I needed to allow my mother to live *her* life on *her* terms and be there to support her along the way as she has always supported me.

Like all of us, I too am a work in progress. Every time I visit Mom now, I think about the tasks I am doing around the house to help her out. There are things I know she appreciates because they are more difficult, yet there are other things I do because I am there and I can. *Those* are the ones I need to let *her* tend to. She still stops me when she sees me overdoing it, but knows my heart is in the right place. Just as we want to do things on our own, so must we allow our loved ones to do things on their own. It is part of being independent.

I had the pleasure of celebrating Independence Day with Mom this year. It made me realize that being independent gives us freedom; and yet so often we hold ourselves captive in our minds by our thoughts and our words. The one who ultimately holds the key is us.

Takeaway

List one example of a time when you stepped in to help a friend or family member and it went south. Did you see the lesson then? Can you see it now? When we are in the midst of chaos, our emotions run high. It's when we become still and quiet that we can reflect and find the answers that lie within. _____

_____

_____

_____

_____

_____

_____

_____

_____

_____

_____

_____

_____

_____

_____

_____

Finding Your Voice

Chapter 11

❦❦❦

THE ROAD AHEAD

"You gain strength, courage and confidence by every experience in which you really stop to look fear in the face. You must do the thing you think you cannot do."
~Eleanor Roosevelt~

As stated in the introduction, I never thought I would be writing a book. I had written dozens of papers in school, sure, but a book? That was a fear I can now say I have successfully conquered. I will continue stretching myself beyond my comfort zone because I know that is where the greatest amount of growth takes place. Life is ever evolving and so am I. I've always said I am a student of life. I believe we all are. The more open we are to learning, the better leaders we can become. Nothing is impossible. The word itself states "I'm possible." There is a world of possibilities out there waiting for you. Remaining open-minded and non-judgmental, not only toward others and for others but for yourselves, will yield the greatest dividends.

I now know the reason I was taken out of life by my illness in 2013 was to be able to step back into life better and stronger than I ever could have imagined, a higher version of myself. It is in this light I can now be that person for others to turn to. Those who feel they have lost their voice in some way, whether physically or metaphorically, I truly know your pain for I have walked in those shoes. Having an attitude of gratitude has helped me through some very tough times. Times I didn't think I would make it out alive, but I did. How? Because I never gave up, and I don't want you to either. Be thankful for what you have in life, rather than what you don't. Live in a mindset of abundance, rather than one of scarcity.

As Oprah Winfrey said: "I know for sure that what we dwell on is who we become." I couldn't agree more. My hope for each of you reading this, is that you become the person you truly want to be, someone you are proud of.

My mission, purpose, passion and vision is to help as many as possible speak their truth and share the voice they have kept silent for so long. June 30, 2019 I was awarded the "All Women Rock" Award in Orange County, California.

Thank you, Marlena Martin, for nominating me and Carl Wilson for this incredible award. I was very humbled to receive it and proud to be amongst the other 49 recipients. I am no different than you. We all have special gifts that we were brought into this world with. The time is now for you to finally Find Your Voice, Unlock Your Chains and Unleash Your Greatness.

Takeaway

List one action you can take right now to get you closer to your dream. You were put on this earth for a reason. You can do this. _____

_____

_____

_____

_____

_____

_____

_____

_____

_____

_____

_____

_____

_____

_____

Finding Your Voice

Renee Reisch

Takeaways

Chapter 1

Think of a time in your life you when you felt overwhelmed or out of control. What physical ailment took place?

Chapter 2

Where are three places in your life you can have more patience? If you can't come up with three, shoot for one. Take a minute to think about this. Be honest.

Chapter 3

Recall a time in your life when you overcame an obstacle? What steps did you take? What was the result?

Chapter 4

Think back to a time when you lost your voice. This may be physically or metaphorically. What happened? How did you resolve the issue (or is it still going on)? Is there something or somewhere in your life where you need help? Do not be afraid to seek support from a specialist. That is why they are called specialists. They have the knowledge and knowhow to take you from point A to point B. Do not hold back. Remember, this exercise is for YOU!

Chapter 5

Think of a time when you promised to change a behavior that was no longer serving you and your old habits came creeping back in. What was the result? This is not a time to berate yourself, we are all human. It is just an exercise for you to see that *you* are in control. No one is running the show but you. If you want to see a change, you are the one who is responsible for making it happen...and you can.

Chapter 6

Recall a time in your life when you wanted to do something but didn't know how it would happen, then by some wonderful twist of fate, it did. This is an exercise on gratitude. Too often we take things for granted and don't truly give thanks for what took place or the blessings we received.

Chapter 7

Recall a time when you felt something was wrongfully taken away from you. How did you feel? What did you do? What was the result? Take this time to seriously reflect upon the situation and write down what took place both emotionally and physically. When we reflect upon situations we were not pleased with, it gives us an opportunity to use each one as a learning experience. Every experience affords growth.

Chapter 8

What is one thing you have wanted to do but haven't because

you didn't think you could? What or who is standing in your way of making it happen? Be aware, the *who* may very well be you. Is there anyone you know to assist you in achieving it? Start making a list of people you know you can reach out to who might be able to help. If you don't know anyone, maybe some of your contacts do. I've had friends connect me via social media with their friends if they didn't have all the answers I needed and I have done the same for them. My point is, there is a way to move forward.

Chapter 9

What was the advice that you gave someone, yet when it happened to you, it suddenly didn't apply? Be brutally honest here. Remember, in order to grow we must own our imperfections and be ok with them. It is part of being human.

Chapter 10

List one example of a time when you stepped in to help out a friend or family member and it went south. Did you see the lesson then? Can you see it now? When we are in the midst of chaos, our emotions run high. It's when we become still and quiet, that we can reflect and find the answers that lie within.

Chapter 11

List one action you can take right now to get you closer to your dream. You were put on this earth for a reason. You can do this.

This book has truly been a labor of love. I continue to grow and evolve every day and this my friends, has been a blessing. Live each day in gratitude, even when you think you have nothing to be grateful for because things may not have gone as you planned. Know there was a reason and a lesson. There is a silver lining in there to be found. As my father always said, "seek and ye shall find." By using the power of my voice, I am now able to help *you* find the power within yours.

I am available for consultations and speaking engagements. I can be reached at renee@reneereisch.com.

Visit my website to schedule your discovery call today at https://reneereisch.com

Follow me on Social Media:

Facebook at https://www.facebook.com/renee.reisch

Instagram https://www.instagram.com/reischrenee/

LinkedIn https://www.linkedin.com/in/reneereisch/

I look forward to sharing my voice with you.

Renee Reisch♥